18.95

WORKERS

EMERGENCY

POLICE

by
Jim Ollhoff

VISIT US AT:
WWW.ABDOPUBLISHING.COM

Published by ABDO Publishing Company, PO Box 398166, Minneapolis, MN 55439.
Copyright ©2013 by Abdo Consulting Group, Inc. International copyrights reserved
in all countries. No part of this book may be reproduced in any form without written
permission from the publisher. ABDO & Daughters™ is a trademark and logo of
ABDO Publishing Company.

Printed in the United States of America, North Mankato, Minnesota.
052012
092012

PRINTED ON RECYCLED PAPER

Editor: John Hamilton
Graphic Design: Sue Hamilton
Cover Design: Neil Klinepier
Cover Photo: iStockphoto
Interior Photos and Illustrations: AP-pgs 6, 7, 8, 9, 10, 11, 15, 16-17, 21, 22, 27 &
32; Carrie Jacobs-pg 26; Corbis-pgs 20 & 23; Glow Images-pgs 19, 24-25, & 29; Getty
Images-pgs 4-5 & 12-13; Thinkstock-pgs 1, 6, 10, 14, 16, 18, 22, 30 & 31.

ABDO Booklinks
To learn more about Emergency Workers, visit ABDO Publishing Company online.
Web sites about Emergency Workers are featured on our Book Links pages. These links
are routinely monitored and updated to provide the most current information available.
Web site: www.abdopublishing.com

Library of Congress Cataloging-in-Publication Data

Ollhoff, Jim, 1959-
  Police / Jim Ollhoff.
    p. cm. -- (Emergency workers)
  Includes index.
  ISBN 978-1-61783-515-5
  1. Police--Juvenile literature. 2. Police--United States--Juvenile literature. I. Title.
  HV7922.O45 2012
  363.20973--dc23
                              2012005976

TABLE OF CONTENTS

POLICE OFFICERS

A police car radio crackles to life. An officer learns that several vehicles have been involved in an accident. Many people may be injured. The police officer's car roars onto the road toward the accident, sirens blaring and lights flashing.

Police officers go to work each day ready for anything. They might have a day where not much happens. Or, they might have a day where they have to protect a crowd from a crazed gunman. They may have to arrest a dangerous criminal. They may have to break up a fight, investigate a break-in, or try to rescue a lost child.

Whatever activity they perform, their goal is always the same: to protect the people in their community. They are constantly in harm's way in order to keep others safe.

A California police officer holds a shotgun and watches for trouble in a nearby crowd.

TO SERVE AND PROTECT

There are many kinds of law enforcement officers who work to keep people safe. There may be several different roles within a law enforcement agency, including detectives, K-9 officers who work with police dogs, and community service officers. Officers have different ranks, depending on their position and responsibilities. Law enforcement officers are assigned to a jurisdiction, which is the area where they have legal authority.

The state patrol, or highway patrol, has jurisdiction on major roadways and interstate highways. They watch for drivers who are being unsafe or aggressive. They watch for cars that are driving at dangerous speeds. If there is an accident on a major highway, the state patrol will investigate. It is likely they will be the first on the scene of an accident, so they may have to give first aid to injured victims. The exact duties of state patrol officers vary from state to state.

In 2004, highway patrol officers are called when a sea lion roamed onto a California road, 300 miles (483 km) from the ocean. The animal was safely captured.

A Kansas police officer poses with Brodie, his K-9 partner.

Police officers are hired by cities and towns. They enforce the laws of their communities. They investigate crimes, respond to calls for help, and arrest criminals. Police officers have jurisdiction only in their own towns. So, a Chicago police officer has jurisdiction in Chicago, but not in New York City.

Rural areas or towns that are too small to have a police force are often served by a county sheriff. Sheriffs are usually elected officials, and they are in charge of deputies who carry out the law enforcement. In counties that have police forces in all areas, the sheriff and deputies may be responsible for the county jail, or provide security in courtrooms. Their jobs vary from county to county and from state to state.

Small rural areas, such as Hettinger County, North Dakota, are served by a county sheriff. The sheriff is elected by area residents. Most states elect their sheriffs every four years.

Members of the Royal Canadian Mounted Police, also known as "Mounties," are on duty on Parliament Hill in Ottawa, Canada.

Sometimes a crime or investigation crosses jurisdictions. A criminal may commit a crime in a city, but then flee to a rural area. In situations like this, the police department and the sheriff's office would cooperate to bring the criminal to justice. Law enforcement officials have to work closely with their counterparts in neighboring areas to uphold the law and keep people safe.

Some countries of the world have national police forces. In Canada, the Royal Canadian Mounted Police provide police services to many areas. The United States has no national police force.

POLICE OFFICER TRAINING

People who want to become police officers need to go to a police academy for training. But first, they must qualify for the academy. They must pass a background check in order to make sure they have not committed a serious crime. They must be in good physical condition, and must have graduated from high school. In many states a college degree is required. Some states require that candidates be at least 18 years old. In other states, they must be 21.

Police academy recruits listen to the Fort Drum, New York, police chief. Trainees spend time in the classroom, as well as in training facilities.

Police students at the North Idaho College in Coeur d'Alene, Idaho, practice drawing mock weapons from their holsters to pass the Idaho Peace Officer Standards and Training requirements.

Police academies are also commonly known as law enforcement training facilities. Sometimes they are part of a college. Other times they are part of a large police department. If accepted, students usually spend six to eight months in training.

Part of police academy training is physical fitness. Police officers may need to chase dangerous criminals, or wrestle them to the ground and place handcuffs on them. The job requires physical endurance and strength, as well as self-defense skills and the ability to protect others.

Students at police academies must also master several skills. They will need to know how to shoot a firearm. They'll need to know how to drive fast, but safely. They'll need to know how to bump a criminal's car to force it to stop. They'll need to know how to help people who require emergency medical care.

Officer trainees also spend time in classrooms. They need to learn the laws of their jurisdiction and surrounding areas. They need to learn what is against the law

Police academy trainees of Baltimore County, Maryland, do push-ups before racing down a beach and entering cold water for a traditional Polar Bear Plunge in January 2011.

and what is appropriate under the law. They need to talk about how to treat people fairly. They need to learn how to investigate accidents. Some recruits even get specialized training in counterterrorism, drug trafficking, or speaking a second language.

After trainees graduate and are hired by a police department, they get even more specialized training. They ride with experienced officers, and a field-training officer goes on calls with them to help them learn real-world policing. It's on-the-job training for the new graduate.

WHERE DO POLICE OFFICERS WORK?

Police officers work in all kinds of places, and do all kinds of work. They often work long hours, and sometimes must work on holidays. Protecting people is a job that must be done whether it is a holiday or not.

Most police officers ride in cars. Some patrol on foot. A few ride motorcycles or bicycles. Some even ride horses. Police officers may work in boats patrolling harbors or rivers. Some officers work in parks or at universities.

Wherever they work, police officers enforce the law. Sometimes they have to catch criminals who are breaking the law or hurting others. Sometimes they have to attend court to give a statement about a criminal they arrested. Sometimes they teach classes in schools about how to avoid dangerous drugs. Police officers have to rely on their training and their judgment, and they count on other members of their team to help them do their job well. Wherever they go, police officers have to be ready for anything.

A mounted police officer patrols the National Mall near the United States Capitol in Washington, DC.

15

EMERGENCY DUTIES

What if police get a call about a multi-car accident, with a tanker truck involved? When the officers arrive, they first make sure the scene is safe for other emergency response teams, like firefighters and medical personnel. They ask questions: What is in the tanker truck? Is it carrying milk or toxic chemicals? Are any power lines down? Is gas spilling onto the road?

If the situation is dangerous, the officers will advise other personnel as needed. If the situation is safe, they will see if anyone is injured.

After any injured people are cared for, the officers must collect evidence and figure out how the accident happened. They may look at tire tracks, draw out the positions of cars, take pictures of the damage from different angles, and talk to witnesses. They have to piece together this information to figure out what happened.

An Arkansas state trooper secures an area after a highway accident resulted in a tanker truck exploding near North Little Rock, Arkansas.

GEAR AND EQUIPMENT

Police officers usually wear uniforms to identify them to the public. They wear bulletproof vests to help protect them from bullets, knives, and small explosions, although if they do get hit with a bullet, they will still receive a blunt force injury. They also typically wear a belt with many tools on it. These tools help them to do their job more effectively.

Perhaps the most noticeable piece of police equipment is the firearm. Most police officers carry a handgun. While officers may often carry a firearm of their choice, some common selections include the Glock 22, Smith & Wesson .45, and the Beretta 92. Officers also carry extra containers of bullets, called magazines.

A police officer wearing a bulletproof vest holds her sidearm as she searches for criminal suspects. A baton is at her side.

Officers also carry a flashlight, with a large, strong lamp. They sometimes need to see in dark places to look for someone who is hiding or injured.

Handcuffs are another important tool. Handcuffs allow officers to subdue dangerous criminals so they have a harder time fighting back.

A baton is a useful tool. It can be used to block an attacker to keep the officer safe, or to knock down doors and windows to reach trapped victims.

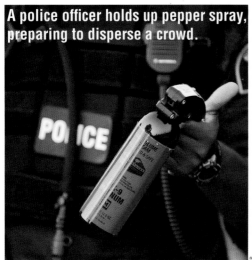
A police officer holds up pepper spray, preparing to disperse a crowd.

Another effective tool is pepper spray. It is a liquid that is irritating to the eyes, nose, and skin. If a person or a crowd is unruly or at risk of becoming dangerous, pepper spray can reduce a person to tears or cause a crowd to disperse. It is not dangerous, but it is painful enough to make people run away instead of doing something illegal.

Many police officers carry electronic control devices (ECDs). Most people call them Tasers, although Taser is only one brand of ECD. An ECD can shoot a projectile that carries an electric charge. When people are struck, they are usually unable to fight back. Police started carrying ECDs in the 1990s. Before that time, police had few options to deal with attackers other than using their firearms. ECDs are considered to be a less-lethal way to stop an attacker.

Some people are critics of ECDs. In the United States, there have been about 300 deaths that have occurred after the use of an ECD. Not all of them were related to the electric shocks, since some of those people had already taken deadly overdoses of drugs or were in other dangerous situations. However, if the alternative is gunfire, it's likely there would have been many more deaths without the use of ECDs. In more than 99 percent of cases, it stops an attacker without permanent injury.

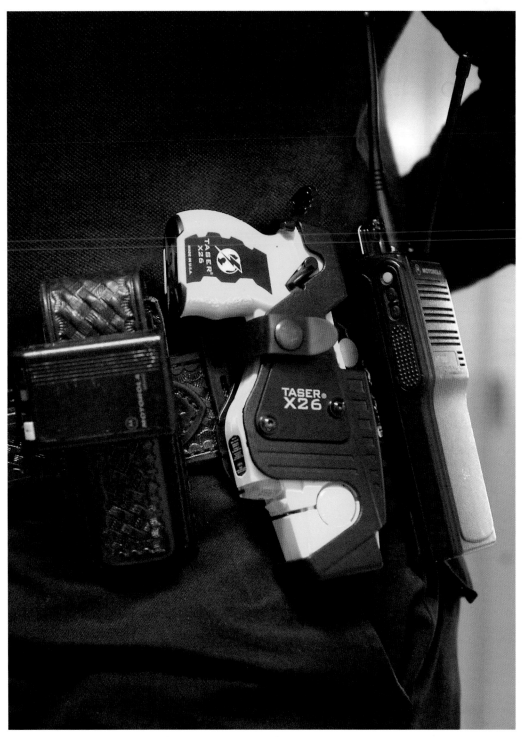

A police officer wears a Taser on her belt. Tasers and other electronic control devices (ECDs) are considered a less-lethal way to stop an attacker.

POLICE CARS

For many years, the traditional police car in the United States was a modified Ford Crown Victoria or similar vehicle. However, today police use many different kinds of cars, SUVs, and larger trucks.

Traditional police cars have larger engines than most cars, so they can be driven at high speeds. They have enhanced electrical systems that generate more electricity to run radios, sirens, lights, and laptop computers. They are built sturdy to drive over rough terrain if necessary.

Two-way radios are standard equipment in police cars, so officers can communicate with their dispatch and with other officers. Certain radio bandwidths are reserved for law enforcement communications.

The Ford Crown Victoria was a standard police car for decades. Many other vehicles are used today.

Police cars are now equipped with computers to allow officers to look up information.

Many police cars are equipped to turn off if someone gets in the driver's seat other than the officer. This prevents someone from stealing a police car when the officer is away chasing a criminal or helping someone.

In the front seat is a laptop computer. With this computer, officers can get immediate records and information about someone. The officer may want to know if a car they are watching is stolen. They may want to find out if a person is wanted by police in another area. They can also record conversations with witnesses or fill out reports while the information is still fresh in their minds.

The division between the front and back seat of a police car is usually bulletproof glass reinforced with a steel mesh. This prevents a criminal in the back seat from attacking the officer in the front seat. Doors won't open from the back seat—they must be opened from the outside. There may be special restraints in the back to secure unruly people.

There is a large trunk for storing equipment, including a shotgun. This is an important firearm that is used when officers feel threatened. Sometimes officers carry special beanbags, which can be fired by the shotgun. These beanbags will knock someone down but not fatally injure them. Officers may carry other guns or rifles as well.

Police cars also carry first aid kits. They may carry defibrillators, which can be used to start a person's heart in case of a heart attack. Police cars can carry whatever officers need for their particular assignments.

After being arrested, a suspect is placed in the back of a police car. There is a division between the front and back seat which keeps a criminal from attacking the officer in the front seat.

INTERVIEW WITH A POLICE OFFICER

Carrie Jacobs began her law enforcement career in 1996 with the Iowa Falls, Iowa, police department. In 2002, she joined the Iowa State University Police Division, where she currently holds the rank of captain and manages the Threat Assessment and Management Unit. She also serves part-time as an Emergency Medical Technician (EMT) for American Medical Response Ambulance Service in Iowa Falls.

Q: How did you get interested in becoming a police officer?

Jacobs: I became interested in police work when I was still in school. I enjoyed the idea of a career that would allow me to help people on many different levels. However, my interest in law enforcement was solidified when I completed my first internship with my hometown police department while in college. Watching the officers respond to individuals in crisis was inspiring. I came away from my internship experience wanting to be that person that others would go to for help.

Q: What's an average day like as a police officer?

Jacobs: A police officer never has the same day twice. The duties of a police officer can vary from traffic enforcement to helping rescue a person from a car crash. Other times, a police officer may be called to present to a class about safety, or help someone find their lost dog. Most of the time, a police officer's day is fairly routine, with little or no danger. However, if an emergency should occur, a police officer is ready to respond.

A police officer helps a man carry his elderly father to safety as Hurricane Ike approaches Galveston, Texas, in 2008.

Q: What's your most memorable experience as a police officer?

Jacobs: There are many great memories. However, there is one event that I will always remember. I was working day shift when a call came into the dispatch center that a man was passed out on the floor of a grocery store. When I arrived at the grocery store, it was evident that the man was not breathing and his heart had stopped beating. I immediately began chest compressions while another police officer on the scene provided emergency breathing. Before the ambulance even arrived at the grocery store, the man started breathing on his own. Within another minute, the man was conscious and asking what happened. My fellow officer and I were told by the ambulance personnel that it was a rare event that a person is saved by CPR alone. There is nothing more rewarding as a police officer than being able to save the life of another person.

Q: What's the best part about being a police officer?

Jacobs: The best part about being a police officer is the opportunity to meet and help a variety of different people. As a university police officer, I have the unique opportunity to meet and interact with a diverse population from all over the world. Paired with the excitement of the unknown that each day brings, I see my job as a police officer as both unique and rewarding.

Q: What advice would you have for someone who wants to be a police officer?

Jacobs: Stay in school and learn everything you can. Most police departments require a four-year college degree for entry-level positions. Do not take education for granted, as it will give you the tools to become a skilled and proactive problem solver. In police work, it is not about physical strength but mental strength and determination.

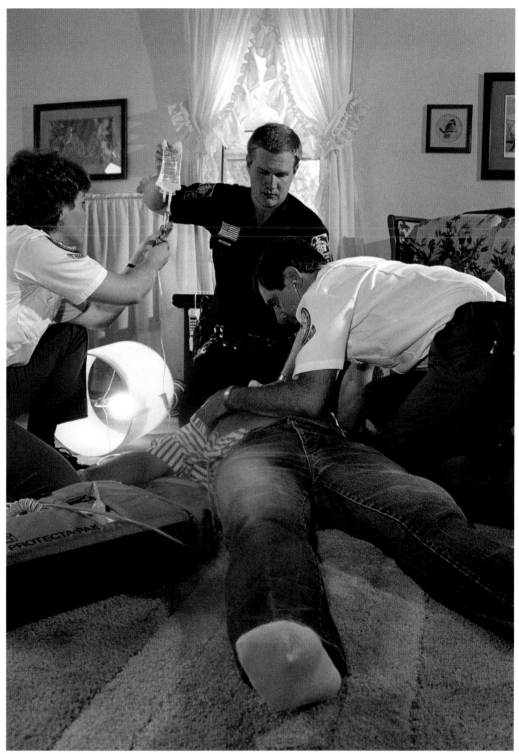

A policeman assists paramedics as they work on a man having a heart attack.

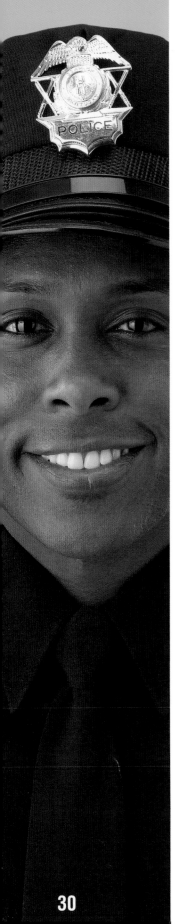

GLOSSARY

BLUNT FORCE INJURY

An injury caused to the body when it is hit, or hits a hard object such as a rock.

COUNTERTERRORISM

To stop terrorists before they can strike. Police work with other U.S. agencies and allies in foreign countries to hunt down terrorists, disrupt their networks, cut off their money supplies, and bring them to justice.

CPR

Cardiopulmonary resuscitation (CPR) is an emergency procedure in which chest compressions and mouth-to-mouth breathing are conducted on a victim whose heart and lungs have stopped working.

DEFIBRILLATOR

An electrical device used to apply a brief shock to a victim and restore a normal heartbeat.

DISPATCH

The people who take incoming radio and telephone calls for police assistance, and dispatch necessary police units. Firefighters and Emergency Medical Technicians also have dispatchers. Dispatchers obtain information and relay it to the officers in the field.

ELECTRONIC CONTROL DEVICE (ECD)

A less-lethal weapon that shocks and immobilizes attackers. A Taser is a type of ECD.

EMERGENCY MEDICAL TECHNICIAN (EMT)

A person trained to provide emergency first aid to victims before and while being taken to a hospital. Also known as a paramedic.

JURISDICTION

The area for which law enforcement officials are responsible, and where they have legal authority.

MAGAZINE

A part of a gun that holds the cartridges (bullets) that will feed into the gun's chamber when it is fired. Police carry extra magazines so that when one is empty, another can quickly be snapped into place and the gun will be ready to fire again.

SHERIFF

Usually an elected official, the sheriff has law enforcement responsibilities across an entire county.

STATE PATROL

Police officers whose jurisdiction includes major highways and interstate highways.

TOXIC

Poisonous or deadly to living things.

INDEX

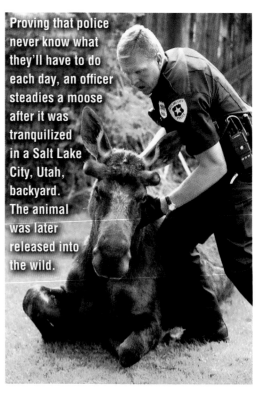

Proving that police never know what they'll have to do each day, an officer steadies a moose after it was tranquilized in a Salt Lake City, Utah, backyard. The animal was later released into the wild.